"My dance is my gateway to the temples of ancient India, to the abode of Shiva, of Devi, of Krishna..."

– *Sohini Roychowdhury*

DANCING
WITH THE
GODS

"To You, with a dance in Your heart – the boy branded effeminate for wanting to learn a dance; to You, the girl forced to choose physics tuitions over dance rehearsals; to You, the 70 year old made to feel too old to swing to the beats in her soul; to You, the young adult forced to forsake dance at the altar of a 'serious' career option; to You, the trans-man stigmatized out of dance; to You, body-shamed into shying away from swaying in public – May this dance be yours – now and forever."

– Sohini Roychowdhury

DANCING WITH THE GODS

An Ode to the Mythological Heritage of Classical Dance

Monidipa Mukherjee

Sutapa Sengupta

SHOWCASE
Roli Books

SHOWCASE

© Sohinimoksha World Dance and
Communications, 2020

ISBN: 978-81-946433-8-8

Published in India by Roli Books
M-75, Greater Kailash II Market
New Delhi-110 048, India.
Phone: ++91-11-40682000
Email: info@rolibooks.com
Website: www.rolibooks.com

Printed and bound in Nutech Print Services - India

MY BODY IS YOUR TEMPLE

The alternately wondering and pleading eyes, the hands folded in prayer, the feet moving as if to a cosmic rhythm, the body a fluid rhapsody of yearning and celebration. This is about dancing with Shiva, seeking to fathom his true identity, to capture his moods, to channel his energy...

This is dance created to bring alive the celestial realm of gods, goddesses with their fascinating stories...

Is the dancer a storyteller? Is that her essential role, her appeal to her audience?

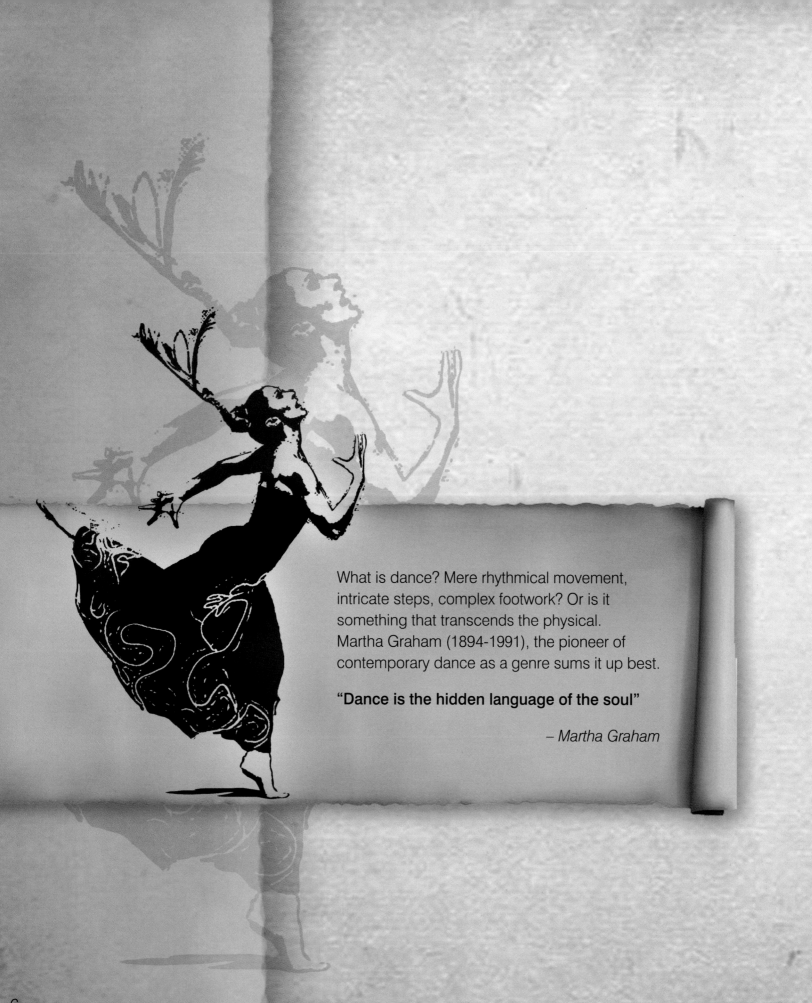

What is dance? Mere rhythmical movement, intricate steps, complex footwork? Or is it something that transcends the physical. Martha Graham (1894-1991), the pioneer of contemporary dance as a genre sums it up best.

"Dance is the hidden language of the soul"

– Martha Graham

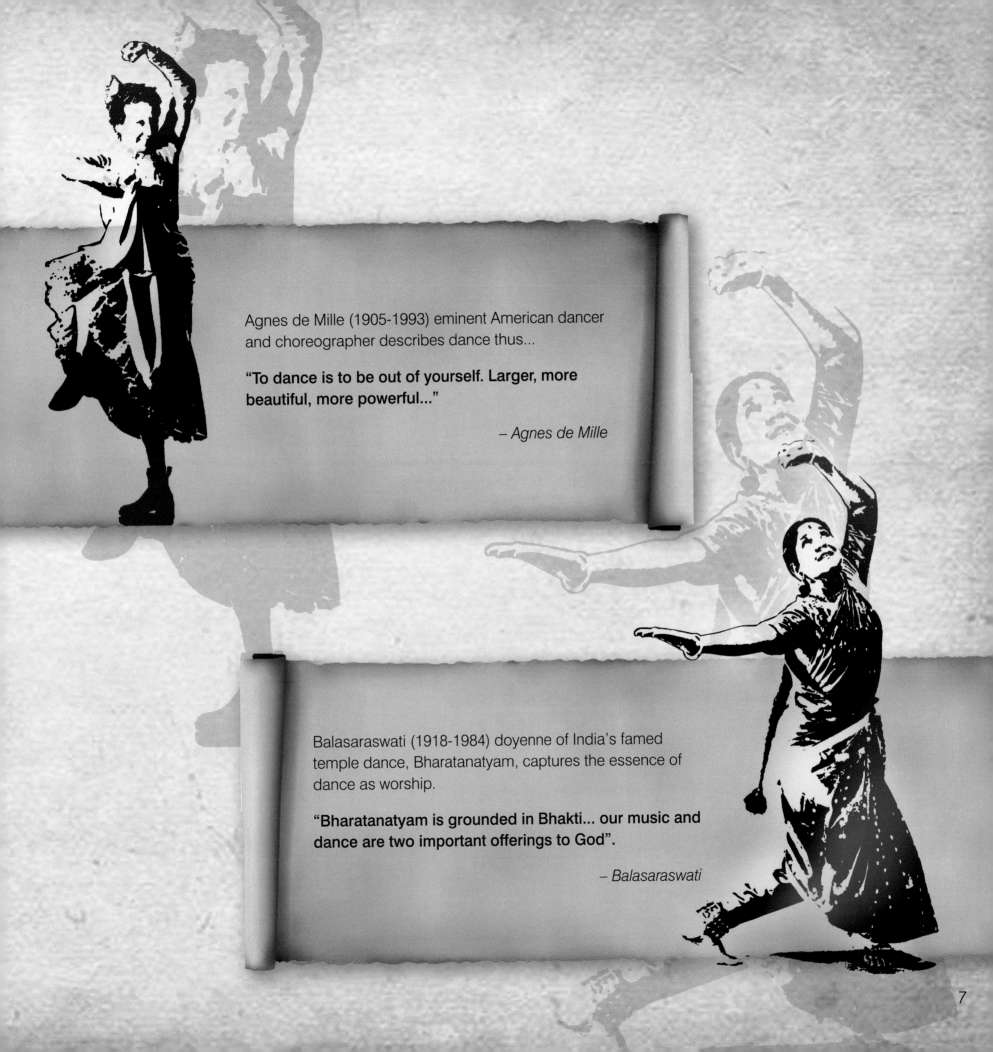

Agnes de Mille (1905-1993) eminent American dancer and choreographer describes dance thus...

"To dance is to be out of yourself. Larger, more beautiful, more powerful..."

– Agnes de Mille

Balasaraswati (1918-1984) doyenne of India's famed temple dance, Bharatanatyam, captures the essence of dance as worship.

"Bharatanatyam is grounded in Bhakti... our music and dance are two important offerings to God".

– Balasaraswati

7

Sohini Roychowdhury, internationally acclaimed dancer and choreographer and founder of Sohinimoksha World Dance & Communications, has her own take on dance as a medium for re-telling, re-interpreting, re-imagining the ancient stories of our gods and goddesses.

"Dance, if you've torn the bandage off. Dance in the middle of the fighting. Dance in your blood. Dance when you're perfectly free..."

– Rumi

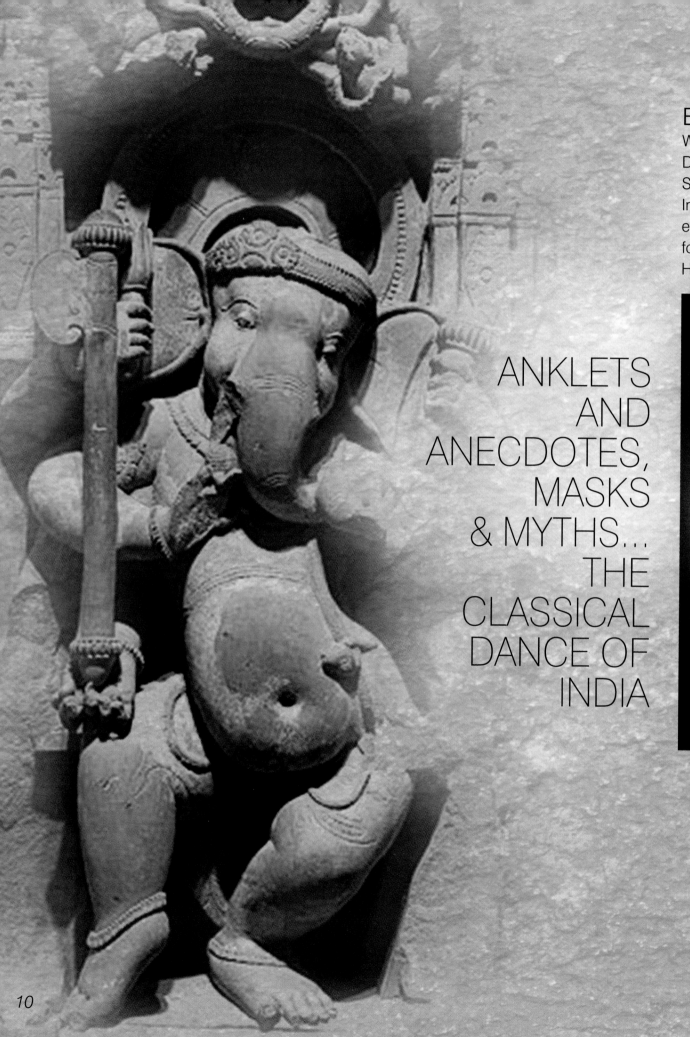

Bharatanatyam

With its origins in the temple dances of Devadasis (handmaidens of God) in Southern India, Bharatanatyam is among India's foremost classical dances, enacting the legends and myths, the forms and moods, of the deities of the Hindu pantheon.

ANKLETS AND ANECDOTES, MASKS & MYTHS... THE CLASSICAL DANCE OF INDIA

Kuchipudi

Originating in Andhra Pradesh, the technique of Kuchipudi is Natya (drama), that includes the twin arts of dance and music, besides acting, to dramatize the tales of gods and goddesses.

Kathakali

Steps and stances used for attacking, parrying, side-stepping and defending, in Kerala's martial arts style, Kalaripayattu, were used later in the dance form of Kathakali, with its signature masks and vigorous dramatic gestures that captivate audiences, as the gods come alive.

Mohiniattam

Kerala's Mohiniattam, deriving its name from two words – Mohini means 'enchantress' and Attam means 'dance' – is a sensuous statement of the feminine identity of devis (goddesses) and apsaras (celestial nymphs).

Odissi

Born in the state of Odisha, in eastern India, Odissi, the oldest surviving dance form of India, as per archaeological evidences, pays tribute to Lord Jagannath through sculpturesque poses and independent movements of body parts.

Manipuri

Manipuri, the classical dance from Manipur, in north-east India, celebrates the cult of Radha and Krishna, and their Raas Leela (nuances of love) is central to its theme.

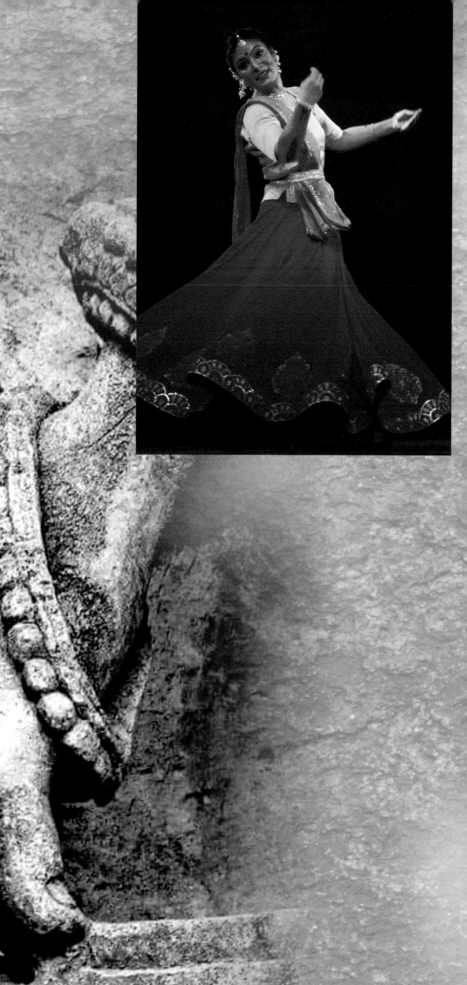

Kathak

Tracing its origins to the ancient bards of northern India, known as Kathakars or storytellers, Kathak evolved to develop two major styles of Gharanas- the Lucknow Gharana and the Jaipur Gharana, patronized by the nawabs of Oudh, the ruler of Banaras and the Kachwaha Rajput kings, often enacting the stories of Radha and Krishna.

Sattriya

Created by the polymath Srimanta Sankardev in 15th century Assam, Sattriya Nrittya, the most recent entrant to the repertoire of Indian classical dances, celebrates the tales of Krishna as an embodiment of Bhakti (divine love).

"O you the creator, you the destroyer, you who sustain and make an end, who in sunlight dance among the birds and the children at play, who at midnight dance among the corpses in the burning grounds, you, Shiva, you dark and terrible Bhairava, you Suchness and Illusion, the Void and All Things, you are the lord of life, and therefore I have brought you flowers; you are the lord of death, and therefore I have brought you my heart— This heart that is now your burning ground. Ignorance there and self shall be consumed with fire. That you may dance, Bhairava, among the ashes. That you may dance, Lord Shiva, in a place of flowers, And I dance with you..."

– *Aldous Huxley*

THE CHOREOGRAPHER OF THE UNIVERSE

The dancer bows to the God of Dance, Nataraja, who is really Shiva performing his Ananda Tandava, unbound, unleashed, vibrating through eternity...

THE LEGEND OF CHIDAMBARAM

Nataraja is said to have manifested near the town of Chidambaram, deep in the forests at the confluence of the rivers Vellar and Cooleron, in the state of Tamil Nadu in South India. In this forest many sages were engrossed in their tapasya (penance), when some of them started practising dark rituals to subjugate the gods. To put an end to this, Mahadeva, came to the forest as a beggar called Bhikshadana. Bhikshadana's beauty so enchanted the wives of the sages that they lost their hearts to him. The furious sages sent serpents and tigers and elephants to destroy the intruder. But the Lord made the serpents adorn his hair and neck. He tore off the tiger skin and wore it as a loincloth. He ripped apart the elephant. Finally the sages created a fearsome demon Apasmara, (also known as Muyalagan), the epitome of ignorance and arrogance. Apasmara confronted the Lord, only to be thrown at his feet, while Mahadeva began his Aananda Tandava or blissful dance of annihilation. Thus was manifested Nataraja, the presiding deity of the legendary temple of Chidambaram.

THE BLISSFUL DANCE DE-CODED

Nataraja of Chidambaram moves to the vigorous rhythm of 'Ananda Tandavam', emanating the eternal energy of

- Srishti – Creation, evolution
- Sthiti – Preservation, support
- Samhara – Destruction, evolution
- Tirobhava – Illusion
- Anugraha – Release, emancipation, grace

The upper left hand holds the Damuru (drum), whose vibrations create the universe.

The upper right hand holds Fire, that symbolizes both destruction and transformation from one state to another.

The lower right hand shows the Abhaya (reassurance) gesture.

The lower left hand is in the Danda (chastisement) gesture.

The left leg holds the Kunchita pada (lifted pose).

The right leg vanquishes the demon Apasmara (or Muyalagan), identified with ignorance and ego.

DID
YOU
KNOW?

Deities who were custodians of dance and music were venerated by ancient civilizations around the world.

As Siwa in Bali, Indonesia

As Bastet in Egypt

As Uzume in Japan

As Terpsichore in Greece

THE DANCER'S SCRIPTURE

yatho hasta thatho drishti.

yatho drishti thathomanah

yatho manahthatho bhaava

yatho bhaavathatho rasa

natyashastra

Synchronization. Of the hands, the gaze, the mind, the thought and feelings. That is what the ancient book of dance, the Fifth Veda, gifted by Brahma, Lord of Creation, teaches the true disciple.

The gods and goddesses prayed to Brahma to create a Fifth Veda that would be easier for ordinary people to comprehend. Thus was created the Panchamveda or Natyaveda. Inspired by the Natyaveda, the ancient sage, Bharata, penned down the Natyashastra. And it became the most comprehensive treatise on the performing arts: dance, drama, music, to endure over centuries.

"I am the demure Parvati, awaiting her beloved Shiva one moment, and the valiant warrior Goddess Durga the next. I am Shiva lost in meditation on top of Mount Kailash one moment, and the furious Mahadeva bent on destruction the next ...I feel transformed as I lose myself in a different Rasa..."

THE DANCER-STORYTELLER'S MAGICAL TRANSFORMATIONS

Natyashastra decodes dance as the power given to humans to channel the changing moods of quixotic celestial beings: Devis, Devas, Apsaras, Asuras, to create magic for the audience… And what empowers them is the art of expressing Bhava, which defines the psychological state, the emotion of the character portrayed by the performer. The nine Rasas are the physical or sensory manifestations of the emotion. The word Rasa is Sanskrit for taste. In fact when Bharata says "Rasyate anena iti rasah" he means that which is relished is Rasa. For after all, life is all about tasting the essence of our deepest wellsprings of emotion.

THE EROTIC
(Shringara)
Presiding deity,
Vishnu

THE COMIC
(Hasyam)
Presiding deity,
Ganesha

31

THE FURIOUS
(Raudram)
Presiding deity,
Rudra

THE PATHETIC
(Karunam)
Presiding deity,
Yama

33

THE ODIOUS
(Bibhatsam)
Presiding deity,
Shiva

THE TERRIBLE
(Bhayanakam)
Presiding deity,
Kala

35

THE HEROIC
(Veeram)
Presiding deity,
Indra

THE MARVELLOUS
(Adbhutam)
Presiding deity, Brahma

THE TRANQUIL
(Shantam)
Presiding deity, Vishnu

VATSALYA
Parental love

The Rasas evolved over time. To Bharatmuni's eight Rasas in the Natyashastra, the Kashmiri scholar and philosopher Abhinavagupta, in his seminal work Abhinavbharati, added a ninth Rasa – Shantam, to complete the Navarasa montage, as we know it today. Also, The Vatsalya and Bhakti sub-Rasas capturing the themes of Krishna and Yashoda, and the devotional love of Mirabai, have added to the dancer's repertoire of emotional nuances.

BHAKTI
Devotion

RASAS WITH THE FLAVOUR OF ANCIENT GREECE

When the Natyashastra was composed (200 BCE), Alexander The Great was in India on his war campaigns. His retinue contained Greek artistes performing tragedies for the entertainment of the troops.

Aristotle's famous law of dramatic unity – time, place and action – as written in his seminal Poetics, is reflected in the Natyashastra, and enacted in Kalidasa's Abhijnana Shakuntalam. The artistic goal of Greek tragedy is catharsis, a purification through expression of the protagonist's emotional journey – something that resonates with the concept of Rasa in Natya (Indian theatre).

THE NINE GREEK MUSES

EUTERPE (lyric poetry – aulos, a Greek flute)

CLIO (history – scroll)

CALLIOPE (epic poetry – writing tablet)

MELPOMENE (tragedy – tragic mask)

THALIA (comedy and pastoral poetry – comic mask)

TERPSICHORE (dance – lyre)

ERATO (love poetry – cithara, a Greek type of lyre)

POLYHYMNIA (sacred poetry – veil)

URANIA (astronomy – globe and compass)

DID
YOU
KNOW?

To transform the dancer into
an embodiment of Rasa,
Natyashastra prescribes

108 karanas or basic dance units

7 movements for eyebrows

32 movements of the feet and hips

24 gestures using one hand

13 gestures using both hands

4 ways of standing

36 types of gaze

9 neck movements

WHEN BODY & SOUL CONVERGE, DANCE BECOMES DRAMA

The finest storyteller holds her audience spellbound by animated gestures, dramatic pauses, vibrant expressions. This is what we need to understand, to fathom the language of Mudra and Abhinaya, which is the essence of our temple dances. After all, the dancer is here to tell us stories about the lives and loves of our gods and goddesses, spanning a vast repertoire of grand emotions. The Mudra is the language of hands, used to define objects and people, birds and animals, gods and demons, moods and feelings. The dancer uses these hand gestures to embellish her Abhinaya, her prowess for drama, as the Nayika (heroine) or Nayak (hero) of the story she is telling. With every fibre of her being.

Abhinaya is the dramatic energy that transcends pure dance of graceful physicality to a performance where the artiste is the actor, the narrator and the dancer. To immerse the audience in the Bhava and Rasa of her repertoire, Natyashastra decodes 4 Kinds of Abhinaya

Angika, where the body, the head, the hands, the feet, all come together to manifest the Bhava through physical expressions

Vachika, where speech and gestures together convey emotions to express Bhava and Rasa

Ahariya, where ornaments, costumes and make-up, add up to create a celestial aura around the performer to mesmerize the audience

Satvika, where the performer's spirit pervades the performance to enable her to channel her inner divinity

"My dance is the coming together of Nritta or the rhythm of the body, Nritya, where rhythm complements expressions through the eyes, lips, hands, and Natya, which is all about Abhinaya or dramatic rendition of stories ...stories of love and battle and rage and peace..."

– Sohini Roychowdhury

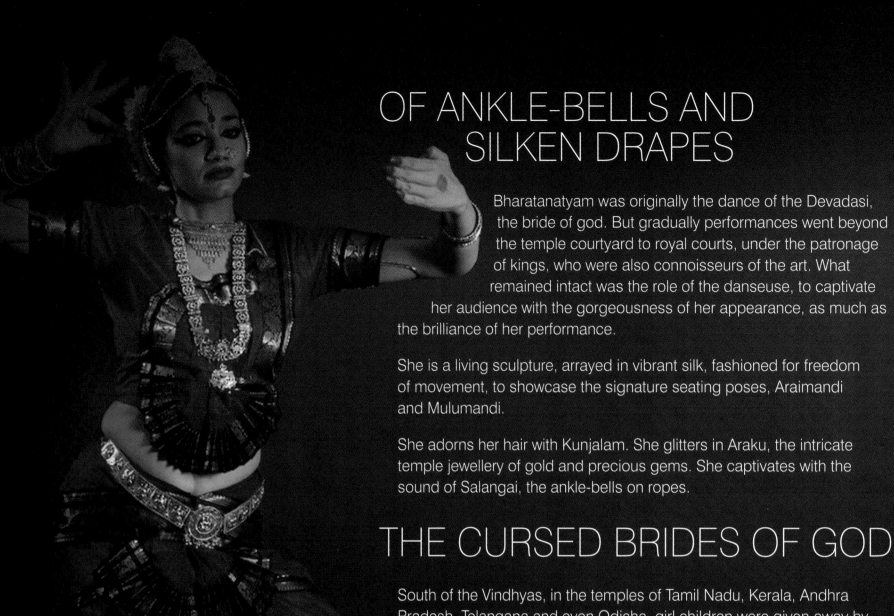

OF ANKLE-BELLS AND SILKEN DRAPES

Bharatanatyam was originally the dance of the Devadasi, the bride of god. But gradually performances went beyond the temple courtyard to royal courts, under the patronage of kings, who were also connoisseurs of the art. What remained intact was the role of the danseuse, to captivate her audience with the gorgeousness of her appearance, as much as the brilliance of her performance.

She is a living sculpture, arrayed in vibrant silk, fashioned for freedom of movement, to showcase the signature seating poses, Araimandi and Mulumandi.

She adorns her hair with Kunjalam. She glitters in Araku, the intricate temple jewellery of gold and precious gems. She captivates with the sound of Salangai, the ankle-bells on ropes.

THE CURSED BRIDES OF GOD

South of the Vindhyas, in the temples of Tamil Nadu, Kerala, Andhra Pradesh, Telangana and even Odisha, girl children were given away by their families to serve the presiding deity as Devadasis. Pottukattu, the dedication ceremony, was somewhat similar to a marriage. These young girls helped with daily temple rituals. Since music and dance were integral to worshipping the deity, these handmaidens of the deity had to learn these performing arts. They were the original heroines, the Nayikas, of the temple dances of ancient India- Bharatanatyam, Kuchipudi and Odissi.

Between the 6th century and 13th century CE, Devadasis enjoyed the patronage of high priests and royalty and were gifted jewellery, land and mansions. They were also highly respected for their art. But with the advent of British colonial rule, the splendour was gradually replaced by squalor. For the Western colonial rulers, influenced by Victorian notions of morality, could not distinguish between these artistes and common prostitutes. But in spite of legislative initiatives to ban the practice, Devadasis continued to serve in the temples, their art forgotten in their struggle to fight poverty and sexual exploitation. Till the practice was legally abolished as late as 1988.

THE EROTIC LEGACY OF THE DEVADASI SANCTIFIED

The origins of Bharatanatyam lay in the Devadasi's dance heritage: Kootu, Cinna Melam, Sadir, Dasi-attam and so on. The Devadasi's position in society, where she had a choice and opportunity as a woman, to work and earn (as an artiste), therefore having to take responsibilities (fiscal) to rear her family, becoming the economic head of her clan and so on, are neither narratives of complete inequality nor complete freedom.

While India was fighting for her freedom from the British and wanted civil liberty in the early part of 1900's, she was also simultaneously sinking in heated debates on the morality of the female performing class, and captured patriarchal and puritanical reform ideas, of ridding the society of licentious women and prostitution, and finally to democratize (for everyone to learn and practise) the arts. As a result, upper class protagonists, notably theosophist, artiste and founder of Kalakshetra School of Dance, Rukmini Devi Arundale, led a crusade against what they termed 'vulgarity and commercialism' of art. The outcome was that the dance of the Devadasis was renamed as Bharatanatyam. Bharatanatyam became a mainstream dance, with a national identity. But it took away the female hereditary privilege that had been the hallmark of the Sadir. The Devadasi system was outlawed under the Prevention of Dedication Act in 1947, in the Madras Presidency. Four decades later, in 1988, the practice was banned in the rest of India.

Caught in a web of multiple political agendas, did the Devadasi end up being dis-enfranchised and discarded for practising her art as a means of livelihood? Did these 'Brides of God' end up being cursed by the dictates of Victorian morality and upper class patriarchy? Did upper class feminist campaigns end up taking away the professional dignity of these artistes, as well as their economic independence, by redefining the Devadasi tradition as a garb for prostitution?

OF DANCE & DIVINITY

"The aesthetics and the artistry of Bharata Natyam alike make us realize that Shringara has a pride of place here."

– Balasaraswati, Doyenne of the Thanjavur Style

From Sadir to Bharatanatyam

The dance of the Devadasi in temples and in the royal courts, was known as Sadir, until early 20th century, when it was christened Bharatanatyam. The name changed, but the dance continues to ignite the divine spark in the dancer, enveloping the accompanying musicians, and the engaged audience as well, in the aura of Bhakti or divine love.

DID YOU KNOW?

The term 'Bharatnatyam' has two connotations – first, Bharata is considered to be the name of a sage-scholar to whom is attributed the first comprehensive treatise on theatre, music and dance, called the Natyashastra; the second connotation breaks up the word Bharata into three syllables: bha for Bhava (emotion), ra for Raga (music) and ta for Tala (rhythm).

The Artiste's Path

The traditional repertoire of Bharatanayam, known as Margam, is the path that the dancer takes in her journey from a novice to the master of her art. The Arangetram is the dancer's debut, when the disciple is ready to showcase her prowess in the different stages of the Margam:

Pushpanjali, where the dancer invokes the deities, for she is nothing without divine blessings.

Alarippu, where the dancer presents the Talas.

Jatiswaram, where the dancer demonstrates her versatile footwork and graceful movements.

Shabdam, where the dancer brings alive a devotional song.

Varnam, where the movements get more complex and challenging as the tempo picks up.

Padam, the most lyrical part of the performance, where the dancer enacts a story of divine love, betrayal and union of celestial lovers.

Tillana, the final section of the performance that demonstrates her dexterity in pure dance, with complex footwork and enchanting poses, that seem to animate the sculpture of India's ancient temples.

Mangalam, a prayer seeking heavenly benedictions with the conclusion of the performance.

Bharatanatyam

Though originating in Tamil Nadu, Bharatnatyam transcended the state borders, and even reached beyond the country. It naturally led to different interpretations by different gurus and exponents. From the pure sensuous fluidity of temple dances to somewhat drill-like movement of more sanitized versions.

Melathur Style

This style is based on Devadasi traditions and Melathur Bhagvata Mela, developed by Mangudi Dorairaja Iyer (1900-1980), centred around complex footwork, and Shringara Rasa. Also known as the Thanjavur style, practised by the inimitable Balasaraswati, this is Bharatanatyam in its purest form, celebrating the affirmation of feminine sexuality.

Pandanalloor Style

This style is attributed to Guru Meenakshi Sundaram Pillai of Pandanalloor, in Thanjavur district of Tamil Nadu, and his son in law Chokkalingam Pillai. It is a purely feminine dance based on Padam or poetry, with deep seating and slow rhythmic movements.

Vazhavoor style

This style was popularized by Ramai Pillai, from the village Vazuvoor in Thanjavur district of Tamil Nadu. It demonstrates a range of fascinating static postures to break the monotony of dance movements, as well as spontaneous Abhinaya, based on rich Shringara and Lasya expressions.

Kalakshetra style

This is a simplified form of Pandanalloor style, introduced by Rukmini Devi Arundale (who was trained in Pandanalloor style). The movements are angular and linear, stiff and controlled, with minimum Lasya and Shringara nuances. Purists often describe this style as dance without soul.

Burning with jealousy, glowing with anticipation, languishing in despair ...the dancer keeps enthralling her audience with the changing demeanour of the Nayika, the heroine of the stories she tells, through her wellsprings of Bhava and Rasa

Svadhinabhartruka
She holds her lover in subjugation, for he is captivated by her beauty and charm.

Virahotkanthita
She is distressed, pining for her lover, who has got diverted by his preoccupations, and not come home as promised.

Vasakasajja
She is arrayed in her finery, eagerly anticipating her lover's return to her bed-chamber.

Kalahantarita
She is jealous and refuses her lover's advances, quarrels and gets heartbroken when he leaves.

Khandita
She is enraged, rebuking her lover for his infidelity, his absence from her bed-chamber, to be in the arms of another.

Proshitabhartruka
She is dejected because her lover has not returned to her on the day he had promised her.

Vipralabdha
She has been deceived by her lover, who has not kept his tryst with her, and she discards her jewels in despair.

Abhisarika
She breaks all inhibitions as she hurries to keep her tryst with her lover, against all odds.

The Ashatanayika is a catalogue of eight emotional states of the Nayika, as laid down by the sage Bharata. To guide the danseuse in her narrative, as much as inspire ancient India's literature, paintings and sculpture.

DID YOU KNOW?

With the onset of the concept of the Mother Goddess, The Ashtanayika was decoded as manifestations of the Devi. Thus the Goddess Durga or Chandi is worshipped as

Mangala

Bhadra

Vijaya

Jayanti

Aparajita

Nandini

Narsimhi

Koumari

53

SHE...THE BOLD AND BEAUTIFUL

Durga

Durga, (Sanskrit: 'the Inaccessible') in Hinduism, a principal form of the Goddess, is also known as Devi and Shakti. According to legend, Durga was created for the slaying of the buffalo demon Mahisasura by Brahma, Vishnu, Shiva, and the lesser gods, who were otherwise powerless to overcome him.

Embodying their collective energy (Shakti), she is both derivative from the male divinities and the true source of their inner power. She is also greater than any of them. Born fully grown and beautiful, Durga presents a fierce menacing form to her enemies. She is usually depicted riding a lion and with 8 or 10 arms, each holding the special weapon of one of the gods, who gave them to her for her battle.

Ishtar

Called the Queen of Heaven by the people of ancient Mesopotamia (modern Iraq), Ishtar was the most important female deity in their pantheon. She shared many aspects with an earlier Sumerian goddess, Inanna. The name Ishtar comes from the Semitic language of the Akkadians, and is used for the goddess from about 2300 BCE.

A multifaceted goddess, Ishtar takes three paramount forms. She is the goddess of love and sexuality, and thus, fertility; she is responsible for all life, but she is never a Mother Goddess. As the Goddess of War, she is often shown winged and bearing arms. Her third aspect is celestial; she is the planet Venus, the morning and evening star.

THE CALL OF THE WILD FEMININE

Kali

In the eyes of westerners, Kali is a goddess, dark of mind, body and soul, a mysterious harbinger of death and destruction. However her story is far more complex and far-reaching; she cannot be easily fitted into a typical western narrative of good verses evil, and in fact transcends both.

She is regarded as the Shakti (power) of Shiva, and he, her consort. She is closely linked with him in many of the Puranas and when she appears in these writings besides Shiva, she plays an opposite role to that of Parvati. While Parvati soothes Shiva, neutralising his destructive tendencies, Kali actively provokes and encourages him. As scholar David Kinsley states, "It is never Kali who tames Siva, but Siva who must calm Kali."

Kali, the high priestess of Tantric rituals, the symbol of raw feminine energy, has over time emerged as an icon of female empowerment.

Santa Sara or Sara La Kali

Sara La Kali, The Black Queen, Saint Sara, Zara The Egyptian, is, every May, the centre of the largest annual Romani Gypsy pilgrimage, venerated by the Roma, who flock to her shrine from around the world. Her identity is surrounded by a few theories:

- She may be the Egyptian servant who accompanied the three Marys (Mary Magdalene, Mary Jacobe and Mary Salome) to France.

- She may be a Romani priestess who greeted them upon their arrival in Provence, France.

- She may be daughter of Mary Magdalene and Jesus Christ.

- She may be the Black Madonna.

- She may be Goddess Isis.

But what fascinates Indian mythologists is the theory that she is actually Goddess Kali, who accompanied the Romani from their origins in India.

"Oh Shiva, I gaze in awe as you dance your **Tandava**, unbound, untamed, leaping like the flames, raging like a tempest…"

"Oh Parvati, I watch mesmerized as you revel in the gentle sensuousness of your **Lasya**, your body moving like the ripples of the lotus pond, the playful springtime breeze…"

And then they danced together, **Shiva and Parvati**, the masculine and feminine principals, as the universe rejoiced.

And then came the moment when Shiva and Shakti, Meenakshi and Sundreshwar, fused their masculine and feminine energies, and the concept of **Ardhanarishwara** emerged. To celebrate the divine spirit that transcends the limitations of sexuality.

The concept of **Ardhanarishwara** is the creative manifestation of the transgender identity. In fact, if we delve into our mythology, we will find it replete with stories around the LGBT theme. In the Bhagavata Puranas, **Vishnu** takes the form of **Mohini**. In the Mahabharata, while **Arjuna** becomes **Brihannala**, **Shikhandini** becomes **Shikhandi**. Yes, our ancients recognized the fluid nature of sexuality, without moral constraints.

'One can become whatever one wants to be if one contemplates on the object of desire with faith.'

– Bhagavad Gita

ONCE UPON A TIME WHEN GODS ROAMED THE EARTH

The temple dancer of ancient times has been transporting us to the enchanted world of India's ancient mythologies. Here goddesses slay demons, gods play truant with their lovers, sages get distracted by celestial nymphs... So many stories from the Vedas, the epics Ramayana and Mahabharata, the Puranas, come to life as the dancer-storyteller weaves a web of emotions and expressions, as she dances her way into the minds and hearts of the audience.

THE TALE OF RADHARANI

"O Radharani, O Queen of Vrindavana,
Your complexion is like molten gold,
Your doe-like eyes are captivatingly restless,
a million full and brilliant moons wane before
Your lustrous countenance and the ambrosia
of Your beautiful lips, red as the bimba fruit, is
life-giving syrup to Krishna."

Sri Prarthana-paddhati by Srila Rupa Goswami

Radha, consort of Lord Krishna, venerated in the Gaudiya Vaishnava traditions of Hinduism as the divine epitome of love and longing, took human form as a Brij Gopika (milkmaid) in Vrindavan. Breaking out of constraints of domesticity, Radha lived only to revel in the melody of the celestial Flute Player.

Symbolized by the Golden Lotus, Radharani, also known as Radhika, Madhavi, Keshavi or Raseshwari, is worshipped as the beloved of Lord Krishna, united for eternity in the realm of Gokula Dham. To some believers, Radha is, in fact, the feminine manifestation of Krishna.

While narrating the story of Radharani, the dancer enacts her playful capers with her Lord and her milkmaid Sakhis (girlfriends) in the woods of Vrindavan. She captures her desolation when her Lord fails to keep their trysts. And as stories unfold, so do layers of Shringara Rasa, as the performer brings alive a lifetime of Bhakti (selfless love) of the human spirit for the divine.

THE TALE OF SHIKHANDI

Feminism, the idea that men and women are equal, is discovered in Hinduism as the scriptures point to the difference between the soul and the flesh.

"The soul has no gender. Gender comes from the flesh".

– Devdutt Pattanaik

The tale of Shikhandi, while lamenting the individual anguish of rejection, humiliation and exploitation of a patriarchal society, also decodes the concept of gender fluidity as a natural phenomenon in India's ancient mythology.

Shikhandi,a warrior who fought in the epic Kurukshetra war of Mahabharata, was born a woman, the princess Amba, who was abducted from her Swayamvara (groom choosing ceremony) by Bhishma, to be the bride of his brother Bichitrabirya. But when she declared her love for Salwa, Bhishma released her. Rejected by Salwa, she came back to Bhishma and asked him to marry her as per Kshatriya traditions. But Bhishma too refused her for he had taken a vow of celibacy.

Determined to avenge her humiliation, Amba spent her life doing penance to be re-born as a man.

Amba was re-born as a girl, Shikhandini, to King Drupad, to be later transformed into a boy, as prophesised by Lord Shiva. When Drupada got his daughter, in the garb of a son, married to the daughter of Hiranyavarna, the king of Dasharna, his true identity was revealed, not only to the chagrin of the girl, her father, but also to Shikandini himself. The agitated Hiranyavarna declared war on Panchala

Distressed by the turn of events, Shikhandini went into the forest to fast unto death, but was saved by a Yaksha (a forest deity), Sthunakarna, who helped him by offering his own gender in exchange of Shikandini's female gender. Thus Shikhandini became the male Shikhandi. After Hiranyavarna's death, Shikhandi returned to swap sexes with the Yaksha, however the Yaksha was cursed by his master, the god Kubera, to remain female until Shikhandi's death. The lament of Shikhandi echoes the dilemma and anguish of the human spirit, trapped in the compulsions of their gender and their sexuality.

THE LEGEND OF SATI & HER VALIDATION BY FIRE

"I am the sacred feminine.

I am the embodiment of the power from where all life flows.

I am Sati, lover and beloved of the Lord..."

The story of Mahadeva and Sati is the reunion between Shiva and AdiShakti. Adi Parashakti again took human birth at the bidding of Lord Brahma with Daksha, son of Brahma, as her father. She came to be known as Sati and Dakshayani. From childhood, Sati, adored the legends of Shiva and grew up an ardent devotee. As a young woman, she forsook the luxuries of her father's house, and retired to the forest to devote herself to austerities. Her resolve finally paid off, as the Lord consented to make her his bride.

An ecstatic Sati returned to her father's home to await her bridegroom, but found her father less than elated by the turn of events. The wedding, however took place and Sati made her home with Shiva in Kailash. Daksha, depicted in legend as an arrogant king, did not get on with his renunciative son-in-law and basically cut his daughter away from her natal family. Daksha organized a Yajna ritual and invited all the gods, goddesses, kings and princes. But he did not invite Shiva and Sati, because he was unhappy that his daughter had married an ash smeared ascetic without trappings of royal splendour. But though uninvited, Sati persuaded Shiva to accompany her to the Yajna. Seeing his daughter and son-in-law, Daksha expressed his displeasure.

Unable to bear the insults Daksha heaped on her husband, Sati was enraged and threw herself onto the fire of the Yajna and let the flames engulf her. Her self immolation unleashed the grief and fury of her Lord, and calamity struck the universe. Shiva took the form of Bhairava, who heaved Sati's body on to his shoulder and began his dance of destruction. Veerabhadra and Rudrakali, potent forces of destruction, emerged from his hair, and wreaked havoc on the Yajna and beheaded Daksha.

Finally Vishnu, responding to the pleas of the gods to stop this destruction of the universe, threw his weapon, the Sudarshana Chakra, to cut the body of Sati into fifty one pieces, to fall on different spots of the earth, that were consequently elevated to Shakti Peetha, or Abode of the Goddess. At this intervention, Shiva calmed down. Daksha was brought back to life, his human head replaced with that of a ram. And Sati was eventually reincarnated as Parvati, who married Shiva once again.

THE LEGEND OF PARVATI, DAUGHTER OF THE MOUNTAIN

'You are the embodiment of Raag Malkauns. You hold within you the midnight calm that alone can temper the Tandava of Mahadeva. By evoking Rasa Shantam, the mood of peace...'

She is Uma or Parvati, born of the Himalaya mountain, beloved of the Lord Shiva. She is the epitome of grace and beauty, the nurturing Mother Goddess, who won the love of her divine consort, Shiva, by practising severe austerities. And she succeeded in transforming the ascetic Kailashnath to the householder Kashi Vishwanath, united in marriage with Parvati, blessed with sons, Kartikeya and Ganesha.

The Shaiva School (worshipping Shiva as supreme deity) of Hinduism tends to look upon Parvati as Shiva's submissive and obedient wife. However, the Shakta School (worshipping Shakti as supreme deity) focusses on Parvati's equality, or even superiority to her consort.

The story of the birth of the ten Mahavidyas (Wisdom Goddesses) of Shakta Tantrism is often told to illustrate this. According to legend, while Shiva is living with Parvati in her father's house, he attempts to walk out on her after an argument. Her rage at Shiva's attempt to walk out manifests in the form of ten terrifying goddesses-Kali, Tara, Tripura Sundari, Bhuvaneshwari, Tripura Bhairavi, Chhinnamasta, Dhumavati, Bagalamukh Matangi and finally Kamala-who block Shiva's exit every time.

Parvati is the ideal wife and mother, the solace and inspiration of her husband. She channels her intellect and sexuality to lead her Lord to experience emotions of reconciliation, interdependence and harmony, playing, quarrelling, debating and loving. She emerges as the balancing energy that resolves the perpetual tension of ascetic and householder traditions of Hinduism, as she complements the raging Tandava of Shiva with the gentle grace of her Lasya rhythms

THE LEGEND OF SHIVA'S
URDHVA TANDAVA

Parvati: What is love?
Shiva: You are love
Parvati: You are mine. I am yours
Shiva: Ever thine. Ever mine. Ever ours...

Kali: What is power?
Shiva: You are power
Kali: You are mine. I am yours
Shiva: Ever thine. Ever mine. Ever ours...

The divine legend of love, where Shiva and Shakti unite across ages, to come alive in the Ananda Tandava, or the Cosmic Dance of Bliss, in Chidambaram.

The legend goes that this dance was a playful duel between the Lord and his divine consort, the Goddess. The Lord emerged victorious by lifting his feet high up in a posture called the Urdhva Tandava, an intrinsic male pose. Unable to replicate the pose, the Goddess acknowledged defeat.

However,another narrative moves from amorous arguments to a battle of egos. Here Goddess Kali, the original guardian of the forest in Thillai, refused to allow Lord Shiva to dance in her place. Lord Shiva therefore challenged her to a dance competition, on the condition that if he won, then she would be banished from the forest.

The competition began with Narada playing the Veena, Nandikeswara playing the drums, and other celestial musicians accompanying with their instruments. Lord Shiva danced with his hair flung in all directions. With the 'Vedas' as his anklets,the serpent as his waist band, the tiger skin as his attire, with the river Ganga and the crescent moon on his crest, he performed the Ananda Tandavam.

At one stage, Lord Shiva took his innate male pose, with his left foot raised above his head, which Goddess Kali could not match. Thus she lost the competition and retreated to the Thillaiamman temple in the northern end of Chidambaram.

According to the interpretation of danseuse Sohini Roychowdhury, there is never any question of defeat. For Mahakali, though unable to repeat the male pose, asserts her feminine power by dancing on the chest of Shiva. Ultimately it's not about a war of the sexes, but rather about the masculine and feminine synchronizing their steps in the Cosmic Dance.

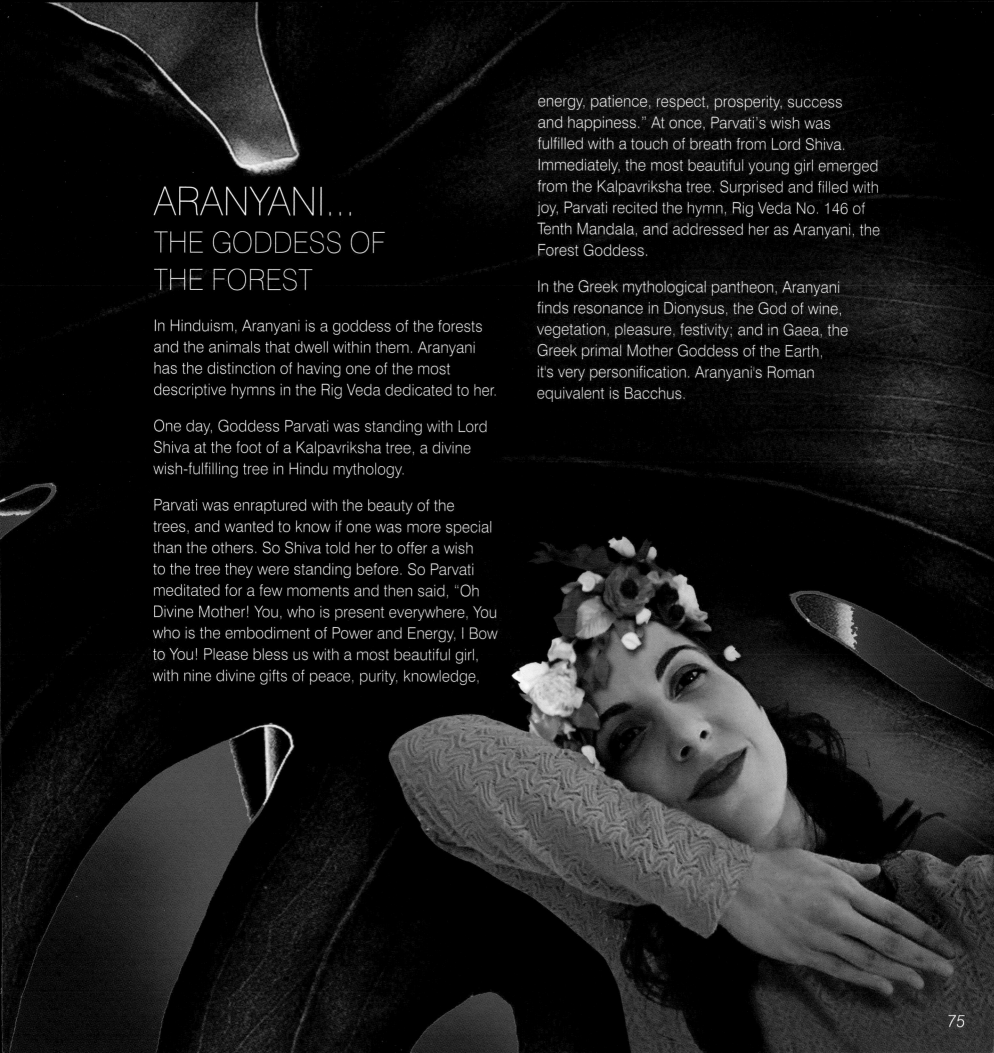

ARANYANI...
THE GODDESS OF
THE FOREST

In Hinduism, Aranyani is a goddess of the forests and the animals that dwell within them. Aranyani has the distinction of having one of the most descriptive hymns in the Rig Veda dedicated to her.

One day, Goddess Parvati was standing with Lord Shiva at the foot of a Kalpavriksha tree, a divine wish-fulfilling tree in Hindu mythology.

Parvati was enraptured with the beauty of the trees, and wanted to know if one was more special than the others. So Shiva told her to offer a wish to the tree they were standing before. So Parvati meditated for a few moments and then said, "Oh Divine Mother! You, who is present everywhere, You who is the embodiment of Power and Energy, I Bow to You! Please bless us with a most beautiful girl, with nine divine gifts of peace, purity, knowledge,

energy, patience, respect, prosperity, success and happiness." At once, Parvati's wish was fulfilled with a touch of breath from Lord Shiva. Immediately, the most beautiful young girl emerged from the Kalpavriksha tree. Surprised and filled with joy, Parvati recited the hymn, Rig Veda No. 146 of Tenth Mandala, and addressed her as Aranyani, the Forest Goddess.

In the Greek mythological pantheon, Aranyani finds resonance in Dionysus, the God of wine, vegetation, pleasure, festivity; and in Gaea, the Greek primal Mother Goddess of the Earth, it's very personification. Aranyani's Roman equivalent is Bacchus.

KARTIKEYA
THE GOD OF WAR

When the five elements of Panch Mahabhoota – Earth, Water, Fire, Air and Ether – governed by Lord Shiva or Panchaanana – the God with five heads, fused with Shakti (Pure Consciousness), Lord Kartikeya or Kartik, the Hindu God of War, was born.

Lord Kartikeya is also regarded as the divine manifestation of the Kundalini Shakti – the primordial, dormant, yet potent energy, said to be present in a coiled form at the base of the human spine.

In Indian mythology from the Puranas, the child Kartikeya is said to have deciphered the true meaning of 'Om', a definition then unknown to his teacher, Lord Brahma, the Creator of the Universe, nor his father, Shiva, the greatest of the Gods. 'Om', the now universally known Hindu chant, was defined by Kartikeya as the repository of entire creation, the vessel that houses the Hindu trinity of Brahma, Vishnu and Shiva, and as that which means everything is unbroken and unshakable love. For this exposition of eternal wisdom from her infant son, Kartikeya's elated mother Parvati, conferred upon him the title of 'Swaminatha' – the Guru (Swami) to her husband and Lord, Shiva (Natha).

And in yet another uncanny correlation between myths and civilisations, Kartikeya's physical depiction is quite similar to the Greek God of War, Ares – they are both armed with a spear!

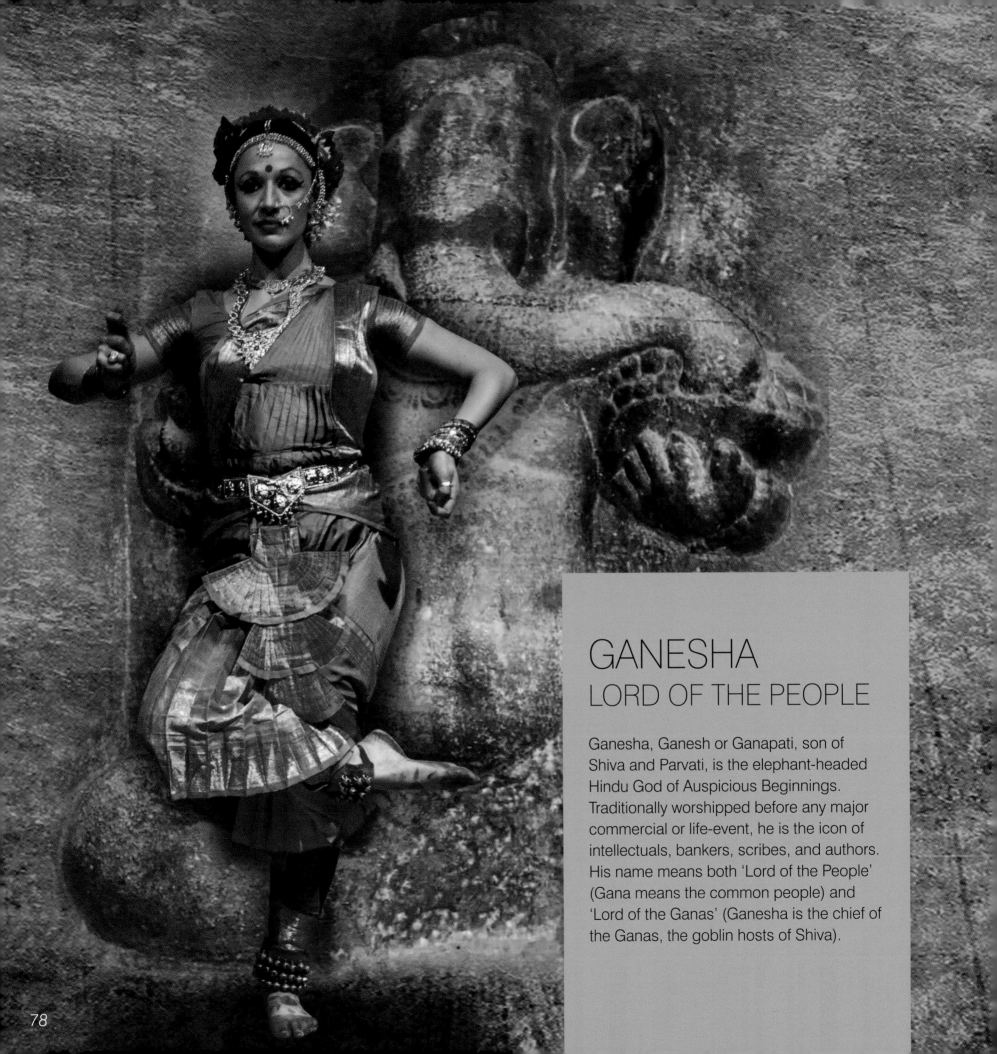

GANESHA
LORD OF THE PEOPLE

Ganesha, Ganesh or Ganapati, son of
Shiva and Parvati, is the elephant-headed
Hindu God of Auspicious Beginnings.
Traditionally worshipped before any major
commercial or life-event, he is the icon of
intellectuals, bankers, scribes, and authors.
His name means both 'Lord of the People'
(Gana means the common people) and
'Lord of the Ganas' (Ganesha is the chief of
the Ganas, the goblin hosts of Shiva).

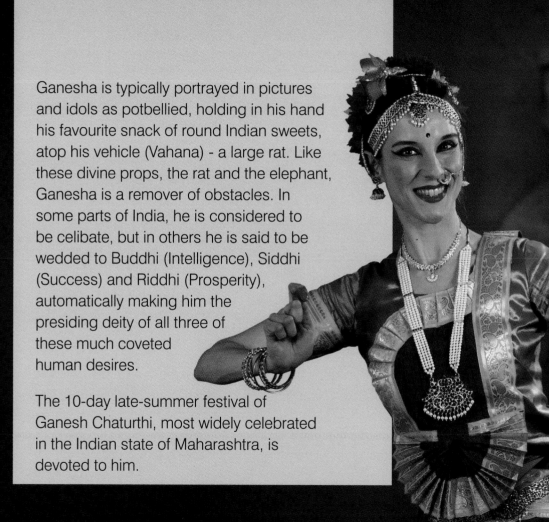

Ganesha is typically portrayed in pictures and idols as potbellied, holding in his hand his favourite snack of round Indian sweets, atop his vehicle (Vahana) - a large rat. Like these divine props, the rat and the elephant, Ganesha is a remover of obstacles. In some parts of India, he is considered to be celibate, but in others he is said to be wedded to Buddhi (Intelligence), Siddhi (Success) and Riddhi (Prosperity), automatically making him the presiding deity of all three of these much coveted human desires.

The 10-day late-summer festival of Ganesh Chaturthi, most widely celebrated in the Indian state of Maharashtra, is devoted to him.

MANASA
THE SNAKE GODDESS

Manasa, the Goddess of Snakes, worshipped primarily in the Indian state of West Bengal and other parts of north-eastern India, is a relatively minor deity in the Hindu pantheon. The goddess for the prevention, and cure, from snakebites, for fertility and general prosperity, she is also revered as the protector of children. Ancient Hindu texts recounting her exploits date back to the 16th-17th century, but she probably owes her genesis to earlier oral traditions. Celebrated through rural songs, dramas and dances, she may be related to the Indian legends of the half-human, half-cobra Nagas. It is believed that it was Lord Krishna who elevated her to full divine status amongst Hindu gods.

According to myth, she is the spawn of the sage Kasyapa, and Kadru, the daughter of the serpent king Sesha. Yet another version of Manasa's birth myth has her as the daughter of Lord Shiva, wherein she was rejected by her father, and later her husband Jagatkru, and hated by her stepmother, Chandi, who scooped out one of her eyes, consequently making her appear to be foul-tempered, and benevolent only towards her devotees.

In idols and images, Manasa is depicted as a graceful lady, her body adorned with snakes, sitting on a lotus or standing on a snake, under a hooded canopy of seven cobras.

Snake goddesses, in some form or other, have existed throughout human history, in legends, fables, cults and religions across the ancient world – with shared powers - to protect, of rebirth, of eternal youth, of resurrection, of immortality, and sometimes, conversely, as a harbinger of death and empyrean vengeance. Manasa can thus rightly claim divine sisterhood, and perhaps some shared genesis, with other serpentine Diosas like the Minoan faïence Snake Goddesses, the Egyptian Cobra Goddess Wadjyt (a personification of the Goddess Kebechet), snake goddesses in Greek fables, Sumerian and Old-Babylonian literature and the Cretan myth of Glaucus - making her a truly global religious icon through the ages.

"Oh Shiva.Let your third eye open within me. So that I can see that the true joy of living lies in empathy,in the openness of spirit embracing diverse life choices, in celebrating inclusivity..."

"I believe that dance teaches us to light the divine spark within us to help manage the struggles and dilemmas of our human existence. And therein lies its power to heal. For my dance therapy initiatives I delve into stories of Shiva or Vishnu or Devi that feel empowering and inspiring..."

Sohini Roychowdhury
Founder, Sohnimoskha World Dance
& Communications

Sohini has used dance therapy for the physical and emotional wellbeing of different groups and communities around the world. She has organized dance workshops for refugee children from war torn countries like Syria, North Korea, Armenia, El Salvador, as well as abandoned children nurtured by NGO's in India, like Little Big Help and Apne Aap. Dance sessions for women jail inmates and their children in Mumbai and Thane, in collaboration with the police in the state of Maharashtra, as well as therapy sessions for disadvantaged children in the states of Rajasthan and West Bengal, are some of her other projects to promote mental wellbeing and positivity among disadvantaged communities. Organizations like Sohinimoksha are demonstrating the healing power of classical Indian dance as a medium for telling stories that inspire and empower.

DANCING INTO THE DIVINE WITHIN

*Search for **Shiva** within you to transcend fear, and embrace the eternal cycle of life and death that connects us all to each other.*

*Search for **Durga** within you, to break free of gender stereotypes imposed by the rules of patriarchy, to empower the self with the will to be a winner.*

Search for **Krishna** within you, the
divine lover, warrior friend and guide
and revel in his Leela ,in the cosmic
play of life and death.

Search for **Vishnu** within you,
*the God who, in his ten avatars,
teaches you the evolution of man,
who has the potential to be the ideal
being, the Purushottam.*

*Search for **Saraswati** within you,
the Goddess of the Arts, of learning
and wisdom, letting imagination
take wing and the mind enlighten.*

The metaphysical form of the Rigvedic
River Saraswati, the Hindu Goddess of
Learning and Music, finds resonance in
other countries of the world as well; as
Thurathadi in Myanmar, Biàncáitin in
China, Benzaiten in Japan, and Yang
Chen Ma, the Goddess of Music, in
Tibet. She is written about as Vagisvari
and Bharati, in the Khmer literature of
the Cambodian Yashobarman era, as
well as in Thai Literature.

*Search for **Lakshmi** within you,
the epitome of grace and beauty,
nurturing the home and hearth
with her gifts of abundance.*

The practice of personifying beauty and
bounty of the Earth as a Goddess, like the
Hindu form of the timeless life-nourishing and
nurturing Mother Goddess Shri-Lakshmi, was
prevalent in all ancient cultures: the Greek
Goddess Core and the Roman Demeter,
both Corn Goddesses, the Egyptian Isis, the
Sumerian Innana, the Babylonian Ishtar, the
Persian Anahita and the Viking Freia.

SOHINI ROYCHOWDHURY AND SOHINIMOKSHA WORLD DANCE & COMMUNICATIONS

This book derives its inspiration, and most of its rare photographs, research, and writings, from the Sohinimoksha World Dance archives.

Based in Madrid, Kolkata and Berlin, Sohinimoksha World Dance & Communications is a multinational dance company founded by Sohini Roychowdhury, an exponent of Bharatanatyam, India's oldest classical dance form. A premier ambassador of Indian culture for the last several years, Sohini's performances in India and across the globe – solo and with her multinational troupe Sohinimoksha, consisting of her students, and dancers, from all over Europe, Latin America, USA and India – have been garnering tumultuous audience appreciation, and rave critical reviews everywhere. Her dedication and special talent as an exponent of Bharatanatyam, her unique choreography and stagecraft, her ability to adapt and fuse the best that the world of international dance and music has to offer, with her classical-dance based choreographies, her culture and language bridging communication skills, have all combined together to create the unique world of Sohinimoksha. Celebrating the Humanism of Rumi, Sufi mysticism, the mesmeric quality of Vedic and Gregorian chants, tracing the cult of the Mother Goddess from its Egyptian roots through pre-Baroque times to the Latin countries to India, the timeless message of Gandhi- all combine in her stagecraft, to underline Sohini's, and Sohinimoksha's, world-view and mission – Connecting Civilizations!

Sohini is a fervent believer in universal Humanism and Empathy, and frequently weaponizes her art, her stage, and her worldview, to help eradicate the many ills and inequalities that plague our society. She is a tireless front-liner in the global wars against poverty, gender-inequalities, LGBT discriminations, child exploitation, sex-trafficking, and education in-access – through her numerous pro-bono initiatives in India, Europe, and South America.

A regular speaker on Natyashastra, Dance, Gender Empowerment, Motivation through the Arts and related topics, Sohini is a visiting Professor at a number of premier Universities and institutes in Europe, the Americas and India. Sohini is a recipient of the Mahatma Gandhi Pravasi Samman by The House of Lords, British Parliament; the Priyadarshini Award for Outstanding Achievement in Arts, New Delhi; Exceptional Women of Excellence Award by the Women Economic Forum, New Delhi; Governor's Commendation for Distinguished World Artiste - by the Governor of Namur Province, Belgium; and has been a European Brand Ambassador for India Tourism's Incredible India campaign.

Sohini has been the 2019 Brand Ambassador for India's foremost saree and accessories brand Satya Paul; for Byloom, one of India's most prestigious handloom and handicrafts brand; and for IAMKHADI, Mahatma Gandhi's fabric of choice, at World Trade centre, Mumbai's 2019 Weaving Peace event.

Press coverage of Sohini's performances, her interviews, and featured articles are published in newspapers, magazines, television channels and websites across the globe, including The Guardian, London; The Times of India; Khaleej Times, Dubai; The Telegraph, India; National Geographic; The Hindustan Times, India; El Mundo, Spain; Times of Oman; El Pais, Spain; The Dawn, Pakistan; Millennium Post, India; Stuttgarter Zietung, Germany; Yahoo News, Spain; Exotica Lifestyle Magazine; The Pioneer, India; Epic TV Channel etc.

Sohini has been called 'a revolutionary in the world of music and dance' by the Hindustan Times and 'remaking history in the footsteps of Uday Shankar' by the Times of India.

SOHINI AND SOHINIMOKSHA WORLD DANCE...THROUGH THE YEARS

- The premiere of Slumdog Millionaire, on the request of its director Danny Boyle – 2009

- Asia Festival Barcelona – 2009

- La Noche en Blanco, Madrid – 2010

- Indian Embassy performances at Madrid, London, Berlin & Moscow – 1996 to 2019

- Times of India Festivals in India – 2016 to 2020

- International Indian Film Academy Awards (IIFA) – Madrid – Inaugural Press Gala – 2016

- Pravasi Bharatiya Divas, Kerala, India (on the invitation of the President of India) – 2013

- National Geographic, Madrid – 1st dance troupe to perform LIVE at this prestigious venue – 2013

- Inner Voyage Event, Dubai – Signature Flamenconatyam themed performance at Inner Voyage event for the ruling Al Maktoum family, Dubai – 2013

- Press Gala to announce the first ever El Clasico Legends exhibition football match between Real Madrid and Barcelona in India – Madrid – 2014

- 1st Indian Dance company to perform at the historic and iconic Cabalgata de Reyes Madrid (Cavalcade of Kings) – leading Europe's largest street parade with 30 performers in front of a live audience of 50,000 and Live TV audience of millions – 2016

- Sohinimoksha performance at the Opening Ceremony of the 29th Maharashtra State Police Games, in front of a live audience of 20,000 – Aurangabad – 2017

- Sohinimoksha performance at the iconic Kala Ghoda Arts Festival, Mumbai, Asia´s largest street festival – 2017 and 2018

- Solo performances for the Tirol County Council across Austria, including UNESCO schools – 1990 to 2019

- Opening Ceremony performance by Sohinimoksha at GRAM Kota and Udaipur, Rajasthan, for Chief Minister Vasundhara Raje Scindia – 2017

- Sohinimoksha performance at the Bloomsbury Festival 2017, London; School of Oriental and African Studies (SOAS) London University; Cambridge University – 2017

- Lecture Demonstrations at various UNESCO schools for Tirol Culture Service, Austria – 2018, 2019

- Bharatanatyam solo performances and Master Classes at Bharatiya Vidya Bhawan, New York, Ananda Ashram, New York; Philadelphia and Washington DC – 2018

- International Advertising Association World Congress 2019 at Grand Hyatt Kochi (Kerala) – Sohinimoksha performance at the Closing Ceremony – 2019

- World Women's Day Conference at World Trade Centre, Mumbai – 2019

- Bharatanatyam Master Classes for the Royal Academy of Fine Arts, Belgium – 2019

- Online in The Time of Corona – A virtual Sohinimoksha production of Dancing with Shiva, to celebrate World Dance Day, broadcast on FB Live from New York - for Bharatiya Vidya Bhawan, New York and The Consulate General of India in New York – 2020

SOHINI ON THE TALK CIRCUIT

A regular speaker on Natyashastra, Dance, Gender Empowerment, Motivation through the Arts and related topics, Sohini is a visiting Professor at a number of universities and institutes in Europe, the Americas and India. Some of her notable presentations have been at:

- Visiting professor - Freie University, Berlin; Leipzig University; Martin-Luther-University Halle-Wittenberg - Germany

- School of Oriental and African Studies (SOAS), University of London

- University of Los Andes, Bogota

- Jawaharlal Nehru Cultural Centre, Moscow

- Complutense University, Madrid

- INK Youth Talks, ICCR Kolkata

- Library Talk at The Tollygunge Club, Kolkata

- Bharatiya Vidya Bhawan, New York

- House of Lords, British Parliament, London

- University of Salamanca, Salamanca, Spain

- UIMP, Santander, Spain

- Casa Asia, Madrid, Spain

- Alfonso X El Sabio University, Madrid, Spain

- UNESCO schools for the Tirol Culture Council, Innsbruck

- Women Leadership Forum of Asia, Mumbai – Keynote Address

Artistes at Sohinimoksha World Dance Troupe

BULGARIA
Kristina Veselinova

FRANCE
Celia Vankeisbelck

INDIA
Harikamal Mazumdar
Jadab Das
Prabir Kayal
Sharmistha Saha
Chandrani Dutta
Deeparna Naskar
Swatilekha Bhowal

IRAQ
Farah Daoud

SPAIN
Maria Sanz
Arabela Diaz
Beatriz H Viloria
Gema Gallego
Olga Mata Gonzalez
Olga Martinez Yuste
Miriam de Castro
Anita Bastida Doncel
Virginia Bastida Doncel
Ester Blanco
Barbara Rasso
Violeta Perez Martinez
Eva Monro
Esther Barruetabena
Concha Caravaca
Cristina Marin

USA
Curline Palmer